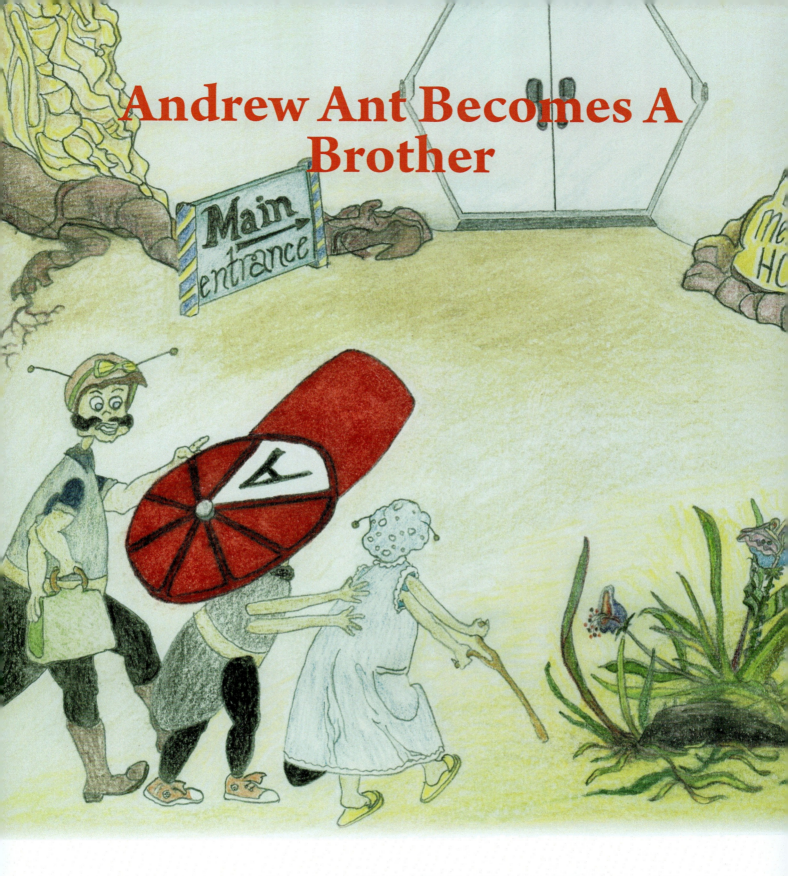

Andrew Ant Becomes A Brother

Written by Glen Ward

Illustrations by Dave Menefee

ISBN: Softcover   978-1-7960-2961-1
         Hardcover   978-1-7960-2960-4
         EBook   978-1-4771-6335-1

Print information available on the last page

Rev. date: 04/24/2019

To order additional copies of this book, contact:
Xlibris
1-888-795-4274
www.Xlibris.com
Orders@Xlibris.com

One morning, Andrew came down stairs.

"Good morning Andrew," Grandma said.

"Hi Grandma, where is mom and dad?" Andrew asked.

"Go sit down and I will tell you." She answered.

Andrew sat down and grandma sat beside him.

"Your mom went into labor last night!" she explained.

"How far is labor?" Andrew asked.

Grandma laughed, "No Andrew, your mom went to have a baby brother or sister for your".

"Really? When can we go see them?" He exclaimed.

"Hold on," Grandma said laughing, "your dad will be home soon, then we will go to the hospital."

"Ok grandma, thanks for jellybean crums they are my favorite."

"I know your welcome". She replied, "When your done go play until your dad gets home."

"OK I will". He answered.

When Andrew was done eating, he put his dishes in the sink and went into the living room. He played with his toys and watched some TV. Time went by so fast.

"Andrew come get some lunch!" Grandma shouted.

"Coming Grandma". Replied Andrew.

Andrew and his grandma were eating lunch when his dad came into the kitchen.

"Where is mom and baby?" Andrew asked. "When can I go see them?"

"Hold on there Andrew, give me a minute to get in the house". His dad said laughing.

"Your mom and baby are at the hospital. I have to get some clothes for your mom, then we will go see them ok?" his dad replied.

"Ok Dad". Answered Andrew.

Then his dad walked out of the room.

"We are going to see Mom and the baby Grandma!" exclaimed Andrew.

"I know, now finish up so we can go". Said Grandma.

Grandma was cleaning off the table when Andrew's dad returned.

"Are you ready Andrew?" His dad asked.

"YES, WE ARE!" exclaimed Andrew, loudly.

"Great, but remember we can't be loud at the hospital, so please use your indoor voice".

"I will Dad, I promise". Answered Andrew.

As they arrived at the hospital, Andrew reads the sign "Beehive Memorial Hospital".

"Great job Andrew. This is also where you were born too", his dad tells him.

"I was? Wow". He answered with amazement.

As they made their way to the door, Andrew met his friend Melanie
butterfly leaving with her family.

"Hi Andrew, what are you doing here?" Melanie asked.

"My mom had a baby, I'm a big brother now." He answered.

"Cool, this is my little brother Arent. He is two". Said Melanie.

"Hi Arent. Nice to meet you". Andrew said, as he went into the hospital.

"Bye Melanie see you after."

"Bye Andrew see you soon". Melanie answered.

As they get on the elevator, Andrew asks. "Can I push the button? Please."
"Ok. Mom is on the second floor". Dad answered.
"Second, that is two right?" He says, as he pushed the button.

As they get off the elevator, Andrew heads to his mom's room ahead of his dad and grandma.

"Hi mom where is the baby?" as he gives her a kiss.

"She is with the nurse. She will be here soon". Mom replies.

Andrew watched the nurse bring the baby in, from behind the door.
"Come see the baby, Andrew". His mom calls to him.
"I'm coming mom". Andrew answered as Dad and Grandma talked to mom.

Andrew walked up to the bed where his mom was holding the baby. "Can I hold her, and give her a kiss?" He asked his mom.
"Not yet Andrew she is too small." His mom replied.
They sat and talked for awhile, then it was time to leave.

As they walked to the elevator, Andrew thought to himself, "Can't hold her, can't kiss her. Being a big brother is not fun at all".

When they got home, Andrew's dad tucked him in bed.
"Get some sleep Bud, big day tomorrow. Baby comes home." His dad tells
him as he kisses him goodnight.
"Love you see you in the morning".
"Love you too dad night." Andrew replies as dad turns off the light.

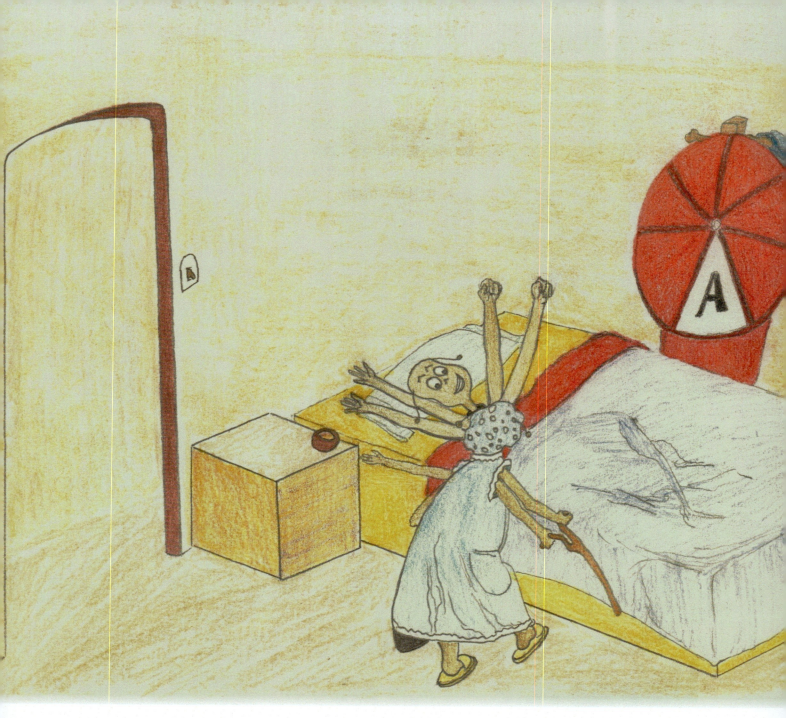

In what seems like only minutes, Andrew's grandma was waking him up. "Andrew, time to get up". His grandma said as she nudged him." Lets get some breakfast before everyone gets home."
"Ok Grandma, I will be right down". He replied.

As they were eating breakfast Mom, Dad and Baby came in the door.
"Your home!" Andrew shouted.
"Shhhh," his parents both say. "Baby is sleeping."
"Sorry, guys." He replied.

As Dad places the baby down, Andrew jumps up and gives his mom a hug.

"I missed you." Andrew tells her.

"I missed you too Andrew". His mom replies.

"Can I hold her now?" he asked.

"Soon Andrew." His dad answers.

They all go into the livingroom, dad puts Andrew's hat behind the coach.

"Ready to hold her?" Mom asked.

"Yes I sure am". Answered Andrew.

As Andrew was holding her, his mom asked, "Do you want to help me bath her?"

Andrew quickly answered, "Yes".

After mom filled the tub, Andrew helped wash the baby.

He played with tub toys.

"Time to rinse her off, Andrew". His mom told him.

"Watch her eyes".

"I will mom". He replied.

After the bath, Mon dried her off. Andrew put powder on her.

"Great job Andrew," his mom said.

"Thanks it was fun". Andrew replied. Just then the baby started to cry.

"She is hungry, do you want to feed her?" mom asked.

"I can, YES!" Andrew exclaimed in excitement.

They came back to the living room, Andrew sat down.
Mom placed they baby in his arms. Grandma brought in the bottle.
"Are you ready? Hold her tight honey." Mom said.
"I am ready Mom, holding her tight." He replied.

Andrew held the baby in his arms tight.

He placed the bottle in her mouth, leaned down and kisses her on the forehead, and whispers in her ear.

"I love you Madison Ant I am your big brother".

Andrew was proud to be a big brother.

Printed in the United States
By Bookmasters